CONTENTS

KV-064-630

INTRODUCTION

Your generation has sat more tests, assessments and exams than any previous generation. At your age, your parents probably only had to suffer one national exam. Because of the qualifications culture at school and beyond today, it is wise to load up on revision and exam tips. Why do it the hard way, when there's an easier way? That's why **learn.co.uk**, the educational resources website, backed by *The Guardian*, compiled advice and tips from experts on the **Revision guide** site.

This book has been developed from the original **Revision guide** material, and has been expanded to include even more revision and exam tips, techniques, and secrets. There's even a chapter on what your parents can do to help you through the exam season – not nag, back off, and stock up on your favourite foods! *Revision Sorted!* will show you the fast

track through revision and how
to keep, not give away marks.
You'll wonder how you survived
without it!

All sites have been rigorously checked for
suitability. However, links often change but are
updated regularly on the site. Visit **learn.co.uk**
for URL updates.

Here are the people whose interviews,
articles and quotes were adapted from
The Guardian's archives for **learn.co.uk's
Revision guide**. Their stuff was so good it had
to appear in this book!

Martyn Berry (Deputy Head of Wilmington
Grammar School for Boys)

Steve Biddulph (Psychologist and author,
who prepared **learn.co.uk's Revision rescue**)

Michele Elliot (Director of the child safety
charity, Kidscape)

Jane Florsham (Senior teacher and educational consultant)

Robert Godber (Head of Wath-on-Dearne Comprehensive, Rotherham)

Hereward Harrison (Policy director for Childline, the children's helpline)

Laurence Hawood (A-level English tutor and editor of *Exambusters* revision tapes)

Peter Loach and Garrett Nagle (Writers for *Guardian Education*)

Daphne Metland (Parent)

Anita Naik (Author of many teen guides, including *The Little Book of Exam Calm*, Hodder Children's Books)

Jim Sweetman (Curriculum expert and writer)

John Wilding (Cognitive psychologist, specialising in student learning)

Chris Williams (Deputy Head of Lincoln Christ's Hospital School)

CHAPTER I

YOU ARE SO IMPORTANT

It is very easy to get this whole exam thing upside-down. Somehow the exams themselves get the starring role when, in fact, you should have top billing. For, without you and your energy, commitment, ambitions and work, exams are just wasted paper.

There are three things that make YOU the most important player in the exam season:

YOUR AMBITIONS

Your ambitions for your future determine how much effort you will put into revising for the exams. So, the first thing you have to decide is – What do I want from the exams? Do you want to be able to study certain subjects, or go to a  particular college or university? Do you want to guarantee your place in a career or job? If your long-term goals are still a bit hazy, then doing better than you've ever done could be your naked ambition.

9

ADVICE FROM THE TOP

Talking to your teachers and careers advisors can raise your expectations. Within the confines of the classroom and the daily timetable and routine, you may have a blinkered perspective on why you're doing the exams. The important thing is to look beyond the exams themselves to college, university or work.

**Advice from Martyn Berry
(Deputy Head)**

Not only is it important for you to sort out your short- and long-term goals, but research has shown that students who write down, read and review their goals regularly do much better at exams and assessments than those who don't.

YOU ARE IN CONTROL

Friends, teachers and family can do loads to help and encourage you, but revising is, in the end, down to you! That's why it is crucial that you are in charge of everything, from your work to your rest. Set yourself priorities and know what subjects are important to your ambitions. Know what to study and how by using revision and learning techniques that suit you. Maintain your health by enjoying a balanced healthy diet, and getting plenty of rest and relaxation.

It's a real boost to your confidence and self-esteem when you are in control and know exactly what you're doing and when you're doing it.

ADVICE FROM THE TOP

"Get a big piece of paper and draw up a plan of action, but make sure it's realistic and achievable. Feeling in control solves 50% of problems."

Laurence Hawood
(Editor of *Exambusters* revision tapes)

Once you have a plan of action, stay on top and in control by ticking off work as you do it. There's nothing more satisfying that seeing a whole column of ticks — just ask any teacher!

YOUR PERSONALITY

Everything about you can be used to make revision and learning easier and more effective. If you're full of beans and raring to go in the morning, that's your time to study. Sleepyheads who don't blossom until the sun is high in the sky, will work best in the afternoon and early evening. Other questions to ask yourself are: Where do you like to work? Do you work best alone or in company? Are you a planner or the muddle-through type? Do the following quick quiz here or at **www.learn.co.uk/revision/** to discover your learning potential.

WHAT KIND OF LEARNER ARE YOU?

Are you an effective learner? Find out in this quick quiz:

1. Do you research, plan and draft an essay before writing it?

   Yes ☐   No ☐

2. Do you revise a topic even if exams are not due for some time?

   Yes ☐   No ☐

3. If you are having problems with a topic, do you discuss them with your teacher?

   Yes ☐   No ☐

4. Do you leave homework until the last possible moment?

Yes ☐   No ☐

5. Do you study at home with the television or radio turned on?

Yes ☐   No ☐

6. Do you read all the comments and corrections a teacher puts on your work?

Yes ☐   No ☐

7. Do you keep a glossary of technical terms for each subject?

Yes ☐   No ☐

8. Do you use a library or learning-resources room to help you with your studies?

Yes ☐   No ☐

9. Have you always kept your homework diary/subject folders/coursework folders up-to-date?

Yes ☐   **No** ☐

10. Can you easily identify the key points of a text when making notes?

Yes ☐   **No** ☐

11. Have you drawn up a timetable for your revision?

Yes ☐   **No** ☐

12. Do you know ways of improving your memory when revising?

Yes ☐   **No** ☐

13. Do you always finish answering every question that you are set in an exam?

Yes ☐   **No** ☐

14. Are you able to forget about schoolwork once you have finished studying for the day?

Yes ☐   No ☐

Your score: 7 or more 'yes' answers

YES!
Consider yourself well on the way to becoming an effective learner. With your skills and this book, you're bound to get top marks!

Your score: 6 or less 'yes' answers

WELL??!
Not a bad score, but not a great one either! You need to focus and use this book to learn how to manage your time and efforts better. You will then feel under less stress and more confident of success.

USING YOUR SENSES

Another thing to discover about yourself is whether you are a visual, auditory or kinesthetic learner. Jane Florsham (Senior teacher and educational consultant) explains what each means and how to use your senses to speed up revision:

Visual learners learn by seeing. Do you need to see information in different forms in order to learn it? If so, then you are probably a visual learner who takes large quantities of information and then presents it in a simplified, but memorable form (e.g. charts, spidergrams, mnemonics). You could put these charts up on your bedroom wall to help memorise them.

Auditory learners learn by hearing. Do you need to hear information in order to learn it? If so, then you may be an auditory learner who listens to ready-made revision aids on tape or CD-Roms to fix ideas into your mind. You could also make your own revision tapes from your notes.

Kinesthetic learners learn by doing. Do you need to do more than just read a textbook to learn something? If so, then you may be a kinesthetic learner who uses muscular feedback and all the senses to reinforce learning. You could create and write revision notes, act out excerpts from a set text, or mime the steps in a science experiment.

TOP TIPS ● ● ● ● ● ● ● ● ● ● ● ● ● ● ● ●

- Write down your ambitions and goals on a piece of paper and always keep them in sight.

- Use **learn.co.uk's revision planner** (**www.learn.co.uk/revisionplanner/**) to email yourself daily reminders of your revision strategy.

- You don't need to spend as much time on stuff you already know well. Identify the topics you don't know and concentrate on those.

ADVICE FROM THE TOP

"Avoid time-wasting and identify weak areas. Gazing numbly at notes or endlessly re-reading them is not study."

Steve Biddulph
(Psychologist and author)

- You are not alone. Should you ever feel that way, you must ask for help from family, friends and teachers.

- The critical thing in doing well in exams is believing in yourself and being confident.

- A little bit of stress during revision and exams can motivate you. Too much stress can be crippling.

- There are lots of revision jobs that can be achieved in as little as five minutes.

ADVICE FROM THE TOP

"Success in life has more to do with being a great person and less to do with school marks than most people think."

Steve Biddulph
(Psychologist and author)

CHAPTER 2

MAKE A DATE IN YOUR DIARY

Before you get into revision mode, it's best to circle a day on your calendar when you can get your head around what you need to do, what you need to get and how you are going to organise yourself. Ideally, this day should be two to three months before your exams start. Diving straight in at the deep end of Ohm's Law, Fibonacci numbers and the Treaty of Versailles without knowing a) if you need to do them, b) how to study them, and c) what to do next, can be time-wasting and frustrating. Instead, get the big picture with an early organising session.

EXAM COUNTDOWN

ADVICE FROM THE TOP

"It is best to begin your programme of revision two or three months before the exams. However late you leave it… devise a revision timetable."

Peter Loach
(from *Guardian Education*)

First, you need a wall calendar, diary, or a comfy seat in front of a computer to visit **learn.co.uk/revisionplanner/**, and a copy of your exam timetable. Fill in the dates and times of each exam and must-do commitments (e.g. coursework deadlines, family celebrations and can't miss parties!).

The amount of time you give to revision is up to you and does depend, in part, on the number of exams and the level of the exams. If you are not sure just how much effort you should (or need to) put in, ask your form tutor, head-of-year, or school's exam co-ordinator.

While you are certainly experienced in the exam routine, your teachers are in a unique position to guide your revision planning. They know your strengths and weaknesses and can estimate how much work and play you can look forward to over the next few months.

TWO TO THREE MONTHS BEFORE

➲ Give your class notes a spring clean to make sure that they are complete and in good order. Paste in all those hand-out notes, finish up assignments and chase friends for their notes on any work missed on days absent from school.

➲ Decide where you will call 'Study Central'. (This doesn't mean on the sofa or on your bed!) You need a proper work space that is:

- well lit and ventilated.

- equipped with a desk and chair that encourages you to sit up, not slouch.

- as quiet as possible. You may be able to work while music from a favourite CD washes over you, but it is hard to ignore the sound of your family watching TV and talking in the next room.

- well stocked with paper, pens, files, stickers, geometry bits, etc. If you've got nice stuff to work with, revision won't seem so bad!

➲ Work out how much revision you need to do by breaking subjects into units or topics. Not every topic has to be revised to the same extent. Some will need a read-through and test session; others will require a more comprehensive revision involving note-taking, extra research, problem solving, essay writing and tests.

At this stage, you should write up lists of topics with the sort of revision each topic requires alongside. List-making sounds tedious, but it is going to put you in control and save you lots of time.

If you register at **www.learn.co.uk/register/**, you will be given your own area called 'My Space' where you can see all the lessons you've done and check the results of any online tests in your very own virtual report card.

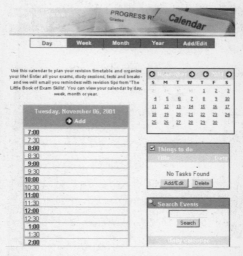

⮕ Making an early start on your organising and revision planning gives you lots of flexibility. It means that if something really important crops up – a manic weekend away, a sports' tournament or a part-time job — you know you can make up the revision time without compromising anything else in your plan. Don't forget if you subscribe to **learn.co.uk**, you can do an hour-by-hour, day-by-day or month-by-month plan using the personalised revision plan, which you find in 'My Space'.

ADVICE FROM THE TOP

"Make up a work revision schedule first. No plan can lead to revision being a waste of time. Planning also helps to get rid of the fear of the unknown, and to give you a sense that you're working towards something. Update your plan daily so that you don't feel ruled by it."

Anita Naik
(Author of many teen guides)

ONE TO TWO MONTHS BEFORE

- Turn your class work into easy-to-follow revision notes. Just writing down the information will help you to understand and remember it! (See Chapter 3 for more about making revision notes.)

- If you get stuck, log on to **www.learn.co.uk**. This site includes thousands of pages of online lessons and tests, as well as links to other useful sites.

- Do a set amount of work each day and take regular breaks. Don't give yourself too much to do – be realistic. There's nothing more dispiriting than never getting to the end of a 'must do' list.

TWO TO FOUR WEEKS BEFORE

⭮ Exams are getting quite close, but that is no reason to go into solitary confinement. As a sense of urgency grows, it is even more important to keep everything in perspective. One of the best ways to do this is to touch base with your mates for group revision and a bit of fun!

⭮ On **learn.co.uk**, there are billions of combinations of randomly generated tests in core subjects, including maths and science (available on subscription). What's more, whether you get the answer right or wrong, it is explained.

If you do make a mistake, you'll get advice on where to find more information on the topic.

⟳ If all this revision is starting to get to you, get some fresh air. A walk in the park or a jog around the block will boost your energy levels.

ADVICE FROM THE TOP

"Your brain uses 20-50% of the oxygen you take in, so in order to keep fatigue at bay, you need to breathe clean, fresh air."

Anita Naik
(*The Little Book of Exam Calm*)

ONE TO TWO WEEKS BEFORE

➲ Summarise your revision even further so that you end up with the crucial information on index cards. (You can buy packs in stationery outlets.) Keep notes short and use lots of keywords, lists and diagrams.

➲ If you get tired or stressed, stop revising for a while, make a cup of tea (though don't go overboard on the caffeine!), read a book, watch TV, have a soak in the bath or do some gentle exercise. Just make sure you go back to work afterwards!

➲ If you're worried about exams or revision, talk to your parents or a teacher.

TOP TIPS • • • • • • • • • • • • • • • • • •

- Dig out as many class tests and assignments as you can to find out just how much you do or don't know, and to spot where you needlessly lost marks first time around.

- Get hold of the syllabus for each subject or course, so that you know exactly what you're supposed to cover. Your school will have copies of the necessary syllabus.

- Give plenty of time to revising tests and past papers.

- Become familiar with what examiners give marks for by checking out **National Curriculum Tests** on **learn.co.uk**.

- Early planning will put you at the front of the queue when it comes to asking teachers for extra help.

- Ask family and relatives to cut out and save for you any revision and exam related articles from newspapers and magazines. As the exam season gets underway, the press rush to give you the latest tips and the best revision aids on all sorts of topics.

- Spend a morning at a local library and check out what resources the staff have set aside for exam revision. Many on-the-ball libraries establish special sections which are loaded with essential texts, study cribs, syllabus guides and collections of past papers.

- If the task of revising seems overwhelming, keep this in mind – How do you eat an elephant? Bit by bit, of course!

CHAPTER 3

REVISION SUSSED

R evision is another word for reviewing. To understand and remember what you have learned, you need to re-read your assignments and essays, class notes, textbooks and set texts. Revision requires accurate notes and careful planning to be most effective.

In short, the aim of revising is to learn something until you KNOW it, UNDERSTAND it, can perform the SKILL and can RECALL it later.

DEAR DIARY

With your calendar or diary in front of you, read the following lucky seven tips and use them to help you slot subject topics into your revision timetable.

1. Keep it short

Revise in short, manageable chunks and take regular breaks. Each revision session should last between 15 and 40 minutes, with 10-minute breaks between each session.

The important thing to discover is what works for YOU. If your attention wanders and your eyes glaze over, then shorter sessions could be better. It may be impossible to revise a really difficult subject requiring total concentration for more than 15 minutes at a time. On the other hand, re-reading set texts would benefit from longer revision sessions.

Get used to breaking your revision periods into minutes – 10 minutes learning French vocabulary, 5 minutes testing yourself on the vocabulary, 5 minutes re-learning the ones you got wrong. Working in minutes gives you an appreciation of how much you can achieve in 'short' amounts of time. This will make you more confident when it comes to allocating time for questions in the exams.

2. Get your priorities straight

Prioritise your workload.
Don't leave the tricky stuff
until last – it may require
more time than you planned
for, and besides you'll just
worry about it.

3. Two-a-day

Try not to revise more than two subjects a
day and don't attempt to do an entire subject
in one go. Sticking to just a couple of subjects
a day (though you may be revising a few
topics from each subject) means that you
won't be overloading yourself.

4. Prime time

Decide what time of day you work most effectively: mornings, afternoons or evenings. Never spend all day studying and never stay up all night hitting the books either.

If you need 10 hours' sleep each night to feel human the next morning, then that's what you need. Suddenly switching to six hours sleep is not going to work. Establish a routine that you can live with, but one that doesn't bore you rigid. If you always find an excuse to put off studying, then establish a set starting time and stick to it.

5. Revise with friends

Forming self-help pairs or groups to assist
your revision and to test each other can be a
great advantage. Working with others helps
you to fill gaps in your understanding or
knowledge and is bound to be more fun than
working alone. But be careful not to make
your sessions all fun and no work!

6. Questions, questions, questions

This is so important – get hold of recent past papers from your school exams officer or subject teachers, or look at the **National Curriculum Tests** on **learn.co.uk**.

Study the past papers and familiarise yourself with the layout of the paper, the types of questions asked, how many questions are compulsory and which offer options. Also study how marks are allocated and if questions are chain linked (the answer  from part one of a question is then required to answer other parts of the question). When that's done, settle down and work through the questions.

If you hit a question that you cannot answer, write down the question NOW and do one or all of the following:

1. Commit yourself to asking the relevant teacher about it at school the next day.

2. Check through class notes and text books to find the topic and then revise it like mad. If you can't find the answer in your books, then go to **learn.co.uk** or refer to a reliable reference book.

3. Phone a friend and ask for help.

Then, write down under the question everything you need to know in order to answer it.

All **learn.co.uk** online lessons in maths and science come with a test. If you are a registered user, you can keep track of which tests you have done and your scores in your own virtual report card in 'My Space'.

7. Chill

ADVICE FROM THE TOP

"Remember to have some fun and let your hair down now and then. Laughter will release your body's endorphins (natural painkillers) and make you feel energised."

Anita Naik
(*The Little Book of Exam Calm*)

"Don't try to sleep straight after revising – your brain will be too active and stop you from getting to sleep."

Jane Florsham
(Senior teacher and educational consultant)

REVISION SKILLS

Take note

Notes help you concentrate and understand a topic. Putting things in your own words is really the first step to understanding and learning. Notes also save you having to re-read an entire subject file.

Make sure your notes are concise (short), easy-to-read, and relevant (keeping to the topic). Once you have completed your notes, rewrite them and keep a final copy stored on index cards or in a small notebook.

The stages in creating an excellent set of revision notes are:

1. Get everything related to one topic together – class notes, assignments, text books, revision guides and reference books.

2. Read through the material and start to take notes under various headings. For history, the headings could be: main characters and their role, where the event occurred, chronology of the event, causes and effects, quotes and sources, etc. Where your class notes fall short, fill the gaps NOW by checking in text and reference books.

3. Read through your notes and start highlighting the vital material that must not be forgotten and also the material that you find hard to recall or understand. You will need to revise these notes a few times before you're ready for the final stage.

4. Shrink those notes to keywords, spidergrams or flow diagrams, so that a whole topic fills only a few small index cards. By this stage, you have revised the material four or five times, so the keywords on the cards act as prompts to remind you of the 'full story'.

ADVICE FROM THE TOP

"It is almost impossible to revise without notes you have made yourself, but it is common to find students wading through textbooks on the day before an exam."

**Jim Sweetman
(Curriculum expert and writer)**

Winning keys

Read through your essays, notes and textbook chapters, and list the main points and keywords under each separate heading as you do so. Keywords can be one or a dozen words that sum up a topic. When a keyword is remembered it will unlock all the associated information.

In your face

Make each set of notes or topic cards really striking and memorable by writing in different

colours, using high-
lighters to make critical
information or headings
stand out. It also helps
to put key details into
colourfully ruled boxes
or to surround them in
stars, hearts and arrows.

Use diagrams

Substitute words wherever possible with
pictures, diagrams and charts. The whole
process of turning words into a diagram
increases your understanding, learning and
memory. Each leg of a spidergram, for
example, has a heading that is linked to the
main body or topic. Make your diagrams and
charts as large as you like, then display them
so that every time you glance at them you
are firmly bedding down the information
and a mental picture of the image into
your memory.

ADVICE FROM THE TOP

"Putting effort, imagination and time into creating a striking set of notes or a diagram is time really well-spent."

(The Little Book of Exam Skills)

Mneu-what's it!??

A mnemonic is a way of helping you remember information using abbreviations, words or phrases. The funnier these are, the better. To remember the colours of the visible spectrum in order, you might use the mnemonic: Richard of York Gave Battle In Vain, using the initial letters of each word (in the right order) to remember the colours red, orange, yellow, green, blue, indigo and violet.

Talk the talk

Oral exams for foreign languages can be more nerve-racking than written exams because they take place in front of teachers, friends and even moderators. Rehearse a number of situations based on previous oral exams. You will have to comment and answer questions on these situations, so learn basic phrases and words that will help you.

Tape-record your 'rehearsals' so that you can evaluate your performance and identify areas that need improving. Careful listening techniques are essential and it will help if you listen to the radio or to tapes in the foreign language for 10-15 minutes each day.

Play teacher

Jane Florsham (Senior teacher and educational consultant) recommends teaching a topic to someone else as a really effective way of learning and also discovering if you have mastered the topic. If you don't understand the material you are pretending to teach then your fake student will spot it and ask embarrassing questions.

Read all about it

To broaden your vocabulary, improve your writing, critical ability and general knowledge, and to appreciate a very important form of communication, Martyn Berry (Deputy Head) advises reading quality newspapers and magazines regularly.

YOU ARE UNIQUE

Before and during revision you will be offered lots of advice about successful learning methods and memory tips. Many of these will work for you. It's not so helpful to compare your revision techniques or progress with others. You and your friends will be working at different rates for different topics. Revision is not a competition to discover who is studying the hardest.

TOP TIPS • • • • • • • • • • • • • • • •

• Studying with friends is a great way to let off steam. Start a mass revision session with 10 minutes of moan and groan.

• It is never too late to start studying, but cramming – staying up the night before an exam and poring over class notes that you haven't look at for a year – is not the smart option.

• Find solutions to any worries – even tiny ones – quickly by talking to friends, family and teachers.

• Give yourself a treat every time you meet a target, achieve a goal or just need to spoil yourself. Studying is hard work, so splash out and be kind to yourself.

- If the whole exam thing starts to totally overwhelm you, just remember that each exam is over in less time than it takes to watch a blockbuster movie or the omnibus edition of *EastEnders*.

CHAPTER 4

STUFF TO TELL YOUR PARENTS

learn.co.uk's Revision guide has been written for students, but it also contains useful advice and tips from education experts, psychologists and teachers for parents. Even though this advice is geared to parents, you are the one who will benefit from their support and encouragement rather than anxious nagging.

During revision and exam time, parents have to tread carefully. They need to give you enough encouragement to achieve challenging goals and your full potential, but without placing you under excessive pressure.

To get this practical advice across to a parent, read through this chapter and circle the best bits. Then recommend this book to your mum or dad as great bedtime reading! Or, you can send your parents to **www.learn.co.uk/ revision/** where they can visit the tips for parents section.

You can also download **Revision rescue** (simply click on the logo to download), which is special advice for parents of 16-year-old boys sitting exams.

HOME
SWEET HOME

What you need during revision and exam time is a calm and totally supportive environment. It is almost impossible to concentrate if your physical space is in uproar or if family troubles cause emotional distress. Sometimes these things are unavoidable, but whenever possible, you and your parents should work together to find the most positive solution. But unless you say something, your parents might not realise how badly affected you are by noisy brothers and sisters, a blaring TV in the next room or by their constant arguing.

SORRY NO BRIBES

This may not be what you want to hear, but head teacher Robert Godber advises that bribes for great results almost always backfire. A really healthy incentive, though, is for your parents to organise something for you to look forward to when the exams are over. The important thing is that this treat is not tied to result expectations.

ADVICE FROM THE TOP

Parents should stay on your side: letting you know their love isn't conditional. They should also try to give extra love and care.

Advice from Daphne Metland (Parent)

GIVE THEM A JOB

Parents often become extremely agitated during revision and exams because they feel they can't help you in a really hands-on, concrete manner.

Attempts to guide your coursework are thwarted by the rules – parents can talk to you about it, drive you to the library and buy you materials, but they mustn't lay a finger on the work itself. When you hit a snag revising maths, many parents own up to finding 'new' maths a total mystery. Despite feeling totally useless, many parents would, if given half a chance, still rather sit the exams themselves than see you go through the grief.

But as so much of the National Curriculum is totally alien to parents, you can enlist a parent's help when it comes to getting organised. They may not understand the details of your work, but as John Wilding (Cognitive psychologist) advises, they can help you plan it. There's loads of material to be sorted, lists to be created and a timetable to compile. Two pairs of hands can make light work of this task, no matter how late in the day you start!

DON'T WORRY – PASS IT ON

Exam stress is as much an issue for parents as it is for you. Within the family, anxiety can be passed from one to another. You start to worry because your mum looks worried; dad gets stressy because both of you are anxious. It is important that your parents handle their anxieties and don't pass them on to you. You've got enough to cope with already without tending to your parents' needs.

You can help your parents relax (and get off your back!) by keeping them informed of what you're doing and how you're getting on. You know how it is with parents – they just like to know!

64

DISCUSS FAILURE

This is a BIG issue and though it sounds very negative to consider failing an exam, talking about it has very positive results.

Policy director for Childline, Herewerd Harrison, recommends that you and your parents should calmly talk through what might happen if something goes pear-shaped with the exam results. It is very important that your parents let you know that it won't be the end of the world and that together you will be able to work things out. This will do a lot to lower your anxiety and pressure levels.

Ignoring the possibility of a bad result doesn't mean it won't happen. Similarly, confronting it doesn't mean you're willing it to happen or that you're lowering your ambitions. Bringing this issue out into the open takes it off your 'worry' list.

ADVICE FROM THE TOP

It is only natural that parents want you to do your best, but it is their job to reassure you that it is not the end of the world if you fail or get bad passes in a few subjects. Exams can always be sat again!

Advice from Anita Naik (Author of many teen books)

You can help your parents by telling them that you will do your best.

BACK OFF

Michele Elliot (Director of the child safety charity, Kidscape) feels that the most important thing is for parents to back off! Your parents know the things that drive you crazy – doing the dishes, picking up clothes, tidying your room, nagging, etc. – so they should avoid these during this time as you are already under a lot of pressure.

An easy way to get this message across is to put up your revision plan where everyone can see it. It won't take your parents too long to realise that you're one busy individual!

NO JOKE HA! HA!

Believe it or not, most parents are totally taken-in by that 'so-what, couldn't-be-bothered' attitude you put on. While your appearance says 'Do I look like I care?', *you* know that inside you're a tad worried about revision and exams. But they don't! Put your parents out of their misery by letting them know that you do in fact take the whole event seriously. Explain that if you didn't see the funny side of this exam business, you could go bonkers! Once done, assume your usual 'so-what' demeanour.

I TOLD YOU SO!

No matter how late you started revising, how little revision you did or how poorly you think you performed in an exam, your parents should not conduct a big post mortem on how you got yourself into this situation. If they do, point out that recriminations aren't going to help, but some positive forward planning and thinking will. It's tea, sympathy, encouragement and a chocolate biscuit you need, not a verbal dressing-down!

IN THE OLD DAYS

When you're feeling stressed, it doesn't help when parents claim that exams used to be harder 'in their day'. Next time someone from an older generation says this, share the following with them:

a) Coursework and modular tests are no easy way out. The current system tests wider areas and more content than a short examination paper ever could. Coursework and modular tests are also weighted quite harshly so that, despite all the work you have to do, they contribute altogether only around one third of the final marks.

b) The National Curriculum and syllabus regulation means that there is now more to be covered in examinations.

c) The curriculum is also rooted in concepts rather than facts. Understanding is what it's all about, not rote-learning.

d) In the 1970s, geography, biology and history – three of the most popular choices at A-level – were all based on recalling one fact after another.

But today, the required level of understanding is equivalent to a degree standard of the 1970s. Geography, for example, requires a grounding in chemistry; and history requires a knowledge of sources, trends and statistics. So the examinations are generally harder.

PARENTS TAKE NOTE

➔ Don't go on at your child about the exams. Being asked how you feel every couple of minutes makes things worse.

➔ Try to listen rather than give advice. Most students describe every exam paper as a total disaster, but parents should refrain from starting an inquest.

➔ Even if your child has been lazy over the past few months, the night before the exam is not the time to bring it up.

➔ Don't organise family visits and days out as entertaining distractions unless you have first checked it out with your child.

➔ Keep in contact with the teachers if you're worried about your child. An apparently stressed child at home may be coping well at school or vice versa.

- Slamming doors, arguing pointlessly and crying are simple safety valves to let off steam. They are not usually a cause for worry.

- If your child is having real difficulty sleeping or is very quiet and withdrawn, then he or she may not be coping well.

- The stress of exams can easily bring unrelated emotional issues and physical complaints to the surface.

- Don't add pressure with comments such as: "You've got to get an A-grade", "Your sister sailed through her exams", or "Your friends are studying much harder than you."

➲ Be lenient about domestic tasks.

➲ If you feel your child is pushing too hard, suggest they take a break. But don't force them to go for a walk in the fresh air because it's something you'd do yourself, says Chris Williams (Deputy Head). "If they're over 18, for example, they might prefer to go to the pub with their mates on a Friday night to relax."

CHAPTER 5

THOROUGHLY TESTED

There's some good news and some bad news. Here's the good news — re-doing old class tests, quizzes and essay assignments, and doing past exam papers is likely to improve your results.

Now, the bad news — they require your energy and commitment. Like lots of other worthwhile things in life, there's a price to pay. If you want a six-pack stomach and a fit body, you'll sacrifice couch potato time and fries for exercise and a wholesome diet. Doing past papers and the rest also needs effort, but the pay-off is great!

PRACTICE MAKES PERFECT

Revision is more than just filling your brain with loads of information that you can retrieve during the exam. It is also about learning how to use what you know. The best way to do this is to complete past tests and exams, and practice papers. With every practice paper you do, you're becoming familiar with the format of the paper and how to allocate your time.

You are also testing that your knowledge is complete and that you can retrieve and use the right pieces of knowledge, understanding and skill at the right time. Practice and more practice with real questions is especially important when it comes to perfecting essay planning and writing.

Though you should try to tackle old papers under exam conditions in one go, you'll also benefit by regularly attempting a few selected questions from past papers. Build time for this into your revision timetable.

THE GOOD NEWS

Here are nine top reasons to put in the DIY testing effort:

1. Doing any sort of test and then checking the answers will quickly highlight material you don't know. You'll also discover just how much you DO know.

2. It doesn't matter whether you are reading, revising your notes, studying with a friend, practising essay planning or reading a set text, always ask yourself questions. Regularly quizzing your knowledge, understanding and skills will immediately prove whether you're on the ball or dozing on the sidelines.

Renaissance artist and all-round genius, Leonardo da Vinci, believed that one of the most important ways of sharpening wits was to ask questions all the time (he must have driven his friends berserk!) and then discover the answers. Self-testing – asking yourself questions about what you've just revised and then giving an answer – is the same thing.

3. During the months before exams, teachers keep you on your toes by increasing the frequency of topic tests. So, if you are already revising and testing yourself at home, then you are halfway prepared for class tests, mocks and module exams.

4. Doing past papers under exam conditions – set time, no help, working at a desk and in total silence – is a huge advantage. You'll become familiar with how the paper is organised, the styles of questions (e.g. multiple choice, short answer, essay) and how much time you should allocate to each question or set of questions. Being confident that you know what to expect in the real paper will cut exam jitters.

5. Test and exam practice gives you and your brain a chance to check how quickly and reliably you can recall a piece of information. Filling your brain with loads of stuff is not enough – you have to be able to retrieve the right bit of knowledge, at the right time. Having the answer pop into your head just as you walk out of the exam is not ideal.

6. DIY testing lets you practise ways of recalling a piece of information that is playing hide-and-seek in your brain. Some find going through the alphabet letter by

letter helps; others use time-place imagery which involves a mental stroll back to the time or place where you learned the information. For more about these and other memory tricks, see Chapter 8.

7. There is a skill in being able to write a well-constructed essay in a relatively short amount of time. And the only way to develop this skill is with practice. Planning is the key. When you haven't the time to write a full essay, then take five minutes to plan an essay.

8. Examiner's have noted that marks are lost because formulae are not used at the right time in the right place. The only way to master this is to work your way through lots of questions, asking yourself what formulae applies and when to use it.

9. Exam success is often about being able to see the simple question which is buried under a seemingly complicated question. This often happens in maths where a straightforward addition and subtraction problem is disguised under layers of scene setting detail at a supermarket check-out. Becoming adept at spotting the real maths in a question takes practice, practice and more practice.

TAKE THE EASY WAY

You know that doing old tests and past papers is a good idea so here are some suggestions to help you make light work of a difficult task.

Do it with a friend

If you are having a study session with a mate, you could agree to study the same topic, then follow up with a quiz that you have both compiled while revising. This is exactly what old Leonardo da Vinci was on about – always ask questions and then work to discover the answers.

Writing essays or essay plans with a study buddy is also one of the easiest ways to discover if you are both on the right track. Both tackle the same question, then swap essays and mark them, noting where you missed an important fact or where the essay plan let you down. The idea of marking each other's work is not to erode confidence, but to see how you can both learn from each other.

Parent power

Getting a parent involved in quizzing you is a great idea. It will give them a job and a glowing sense of satisfaction. It's also handy that you can get their help at a moment's notice.

Parents are especially good at quick-fire quizzes where there is only one right answer (e.g. mental maths, spelling or language vocabulary). Avoid the sorts of questions and answers where concepts and interpretation are involved – you want their help, not an argument or lecture starting with the words "In my day…".

Off the shelf

Year-round, the shelves in bookshops and newsagents groan under the weight of revision aids. Among all these books you will find ones brimming with questions on every subject topic under the sun. They are incredibly useful and easy to use, so agree with friends which ones you all need and then arrange to buy different ones and circulate them between you.

If you can't always find the time to complete a full past paper, then work through it bit by bit. Only one word of advice — don't skip the nasty questions!

Use the Internet

On sites like **learn.co.uk**, you will find the most recent past papers as well as online tests and topic quizzes. Here's a brief example of what you can expect in an online KS3 maths quiz on the topic of roots, levels 3-6:

What is $\sqrt[3]{216}$?

6

Once you have answered all the questions, submit your answers for marking. Your answers will come back to you marked and the working out shown or the answer explained. Here's the working out to the first question:

Answer: 6

Comment

$\sqrt[3]{216} = \sqrt[3]{6 \times 6 \times 6}$
$\phantom{\sqrt[3]{216}} = 6$

And from KS4 science, here's one of the **learn.co.uk** question/answer sequences on the topic of reproduction:

?

Question: If fruits and seeds are light, and have flattened wings or parachutes to provide a large surface area to increase buoyancy in the air, they are probably dispersed by:

Choose one: water animals birds air insects

Answer: air

Comment: The features described are adaptations by fruit and seeds to be dispersed by air. They will be blown by the wind to places as far as possible from the parent plant where they are able to germinate into new plants.

Online tests are quick to do and feedback is immediate and comprehensive. If you scored badly or missed a question, you can take the test again by simply clicking the browser's back button and REFRESH the page.

learn.co.uk can also help you to keep tabs on the lessons, activities, quizzes and tests you have done, as well as how you fared. All you have to do is register and then log-in every time you visit the site.

Online lessons, tests and activities at
learn.co.uk will ultimately cover the entire
National Curriculum from KS1 to A-level. You
can access the lessons by clicking on 'Online
lessons' on the home page, and then clicking
on the right level and subject. Once into the
subject, choose a topic and click your way
to exam success.

CHAPTER 6

FUII MARKS!

As day one of the exams draws close, your most desperate desire is to get the exams over and done with. In the headlong race to the finish it is easy to forget your ambition of achieving a level 6 in English or an A* in physics. Suddenly, earning marks to achieve a grade isn't half as important as simply surviving the next few weeks. But now is the time to really keep your cool so that YOU keep every mark.

MARKING SYSTEMS

There is nothing random about how papers are marked. Each question is allocated a set amount of marks and to achieve all those marks you must give a full answer. What constitutes a full answer is established in the marking schemes. All examiners work within these marking schemes.

This chapter includes an example of an examiner's comments and a model answer to a specific type of question. If you want to look at more examples, go to **www.learn.co.uk/revision/**

EXAM TECHNIQUE

Twelve tried and tested tips to keep you cool and on the right side of the examiner:

1. Examiners are not mind-readers

In an exam, you are being asked to communicate – examiners cannot read your mind. For example, you may think something is obvious, but you must still share it with the examiner, otherwise he or she cannot know what you are thinking. You will not be given any credit for something that you have not shown or written on the paper.

2. Examiners know nothing

When preparing an answer, especially an essay response to a question, it's best to imagine that the examiner knows nothing about the topic. Your answer therefore has to be totally clear and contain all the information to bring the examiner up to speed.

When quoting a figure from history – even a mega famous one – don't just write the name of the source. Go one step further and explain who he or she was and put the figure into context. For example, when quoting Winston Churchill, introduce the quote with 'Sir Winston Churchill speaking as First Lord of Admiralty at the outbreak of World War One'. Details like this really show the examiner that you know your stuff.

3. Examiners are not code-breakers

Make sure your handwriting is easy to read and your presentation is clear so that the examiner can spot every mark you have earned. Don't lose marks simply because the examiner can't decipher messy writing or diagrams.

4. Read the question

Don't rush into answering a question after a quick read-through, no matter how confident you are about the answer. Take a breath, read the question again carefully, noting keywords in the question, and follow the instructions precisely. Misreading a keyword might result in a totally wrong answer and not following an instruction to 'illustrate with examples' or to 'put one cross in a box' may also mean marks down the drain.

5. Answer the question asked

This seems really obvious but it happens so often. An answer starts on the right track but loses its way; or sometimes an answer goes all round the topic, but never actually hits the target. These problems are caused by jumping in too quickly and poor planning. To start with, give yourself a chance to read the entire paper, then read each question twice before putting pen to paper. It is better to spend five seconds checking a question and your planning, than five minutes doing the wrong thing.

6. Show working out

If your final answer is wrong, in a maths question, for example, the examiner can check your working out to see if you understood the question and had the knowledge and skill to do it. If your working out shows any of these, then you may gain a proportion of the marks allocated to that question.

7. Keep it simple

Even when writing essay answers, don't be
suddenly tempted to go on a literary
experiment into strange punctuation, unfamiliar
or exaggerated language, complicated
sentences or long-winded paragraphs. Keep
your meaning and purpose clear.

ADVICE FROM THE TOP

*"Keep sentences short by sticking to
the one fact per sentence rule. Keep
essays punchy by dealing with one
idea per paragraph."*

(The Little Book of Exam Skills)

103

8. Never leave a blank

Always provide an answer to every question. You may guess at an answer, but even a shot in the dark can earn marks.

9. Have a strategy

Before you go into the exam, decide what
you will do if you hit a nasty question. You
may feel more comfortable attempting to
answer it there and then so that you are not
worrying about it while you do the rest of the
paper. Or you may be happier putting a mark
alongside the troublesome question and
returning to it later.

10. Don't get bogged down

If you get stuck halfway into an answer or have wandered off the point, stop immediately and put your pen down. It may be best to move onto the next question, especially if you have used up the time allocated to that question. What you must avoid is getting into a blind panic that will sap your confidence and use up time that would be better spent on other questions. Check out Chapter 7 for quick relaxation tips.

11. Clock watcher

Stick to your time allocations for each
question as closely as possible. It would be
a waste spending half the exam time on a
question worth only 10% of the marks.

12. Checking out

Allow time to check over your paper at the
end. Use this time to make sure you've
answered all necessary questions and to read
through answers for spelling, grammar, facts
and workings out. Take care in exams where
marks can be deducted for poor spelling
and grammar.

SPOT ON TECHNIQUES

How can you get the most marks for specific types of questions? Garrett Nagle and Peter Loach (from *Guardian Education*) have selected a few prime examples of how to approach certain questions. Even if the subjects or level of work is outside of your current curriculum, the examiner's comments and observations are full of valuable advice for all students.

Turning the tables

Many subjects, such as geography, biology, PE and maths use tables of data in exams for data response or data stimulus questions. These questions ask you to make clear and to-the-point comments about a set of information.

The first things you look for in the data or graph are the highest and lowest values (maximum and minimum), the trend or general pattern, and any exceptions. Even if the information supplied doesn't show all the features, if you keep these in mind, you will get the correct answer across to the examiner.

ADVICE FROM THE TOP

"You should use the data to support your answer. This means that you must name names and quote figures."

Garrett Nagle
(from *Guardian Education*)

Here is an example of a data-related question, and a student's answer and the examiner's comment. If you follow this carefully, you will discover what it takes to get full marks. If you would like to check out more data tables and read all the questions in full, go to:
www.learn.co.uk/revision/

Exam question: Which foods provide most protein and which provide most carbohydrates? Is there any pattern that you can see?

(5 marks)

Data supplied with question:

Composition of food
Per 100g

	Jam	Honey	Marmite	Cheese	Tuna paste
Energy (calories)	266	322	886	410	237
Protein (g)	0.3	0.4	45.0	25.0	17.0
Carbohydrate (g)	66.0	80.0	7.0	0.1	0.1

Answer: Marmite, cheese and tuna paste are all good sources of protein. Marmite contains the largest by far, but even tuna paste contains about 40 times as much protein per 100g as does sugar or honey. By contrast, jam and honey, which are very low in protein, are very high in carbohydrates (66g per 100g and 80g per 100g) whereas Marmite (7g per 100g) cheese and tuna paste (both 0.1g per 100g) are low in carbohydrates. Thus, the foods with a lot of protein contain few carbohydrates whereas those rich in carbohydrates have small amounts of protein.

Examiner's comment: This question is worth 5 marks. Sometimes we may look for 5 points or better still 3 points supported with evidence from the table. Here the student has identified the basic difference between the quality foods (cheese and Marmite) and the quantity or energy foods (jam and honey). She has used data to support her answer and uses words and phrases such as 'by contrast', and 'thus'. There is a real feeling that the student is on top of the subject and has communicated this clearly to me. 5/5 – full marks!

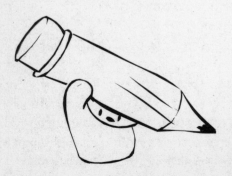

Spot the keyword

In any exam, the type of answer you give depends on the question you are asked. For example, the question may ask you to list, describe, explain or evaluate.

Question 1: *For an urban area that you have studied,* **list** *the factors that make it vulnerable to flooding.*

Answer: Provide only a list of points (rather than full sentences) as the answer. If you mis-read the keyword ('list') you may have lost marks.

Question 2: Describe *the flood problem in an urban area that you have studied.*

Answer: This question requires more detail and the use of local information. It is also asking for full sentences.

? *Question 3:* **Explain** *the flood problem for an urban area that you have studied.*

Answer: This requires an explanation, examples and full sentences.

? *Question 4:* **Evaluate** *the problem of flooding in Oxford.*

Answer: This question asks you to compare the problem of flooding in Oxford with other areas, and to assess how important flooding is in Oxford.

(Full answers can be found in the **learn.co.uk Revision guide**.)

CASE STUDIES

A case study is a detailed, real example of what you have studied (e.g. a village, farm, region or country). When you mention case studies in an exam make sure you use a real example – give its name and location – and an example which shows the points you are trying to make.

Revise a number of case studies of different scales or size – local, regional and national – so that you are well-prepared to answer questions.

Certain phrases in exam questions are cues for you to use your case study in your answer. Here are some examples of these phrases:

"Using an example from your studies..."

"With reference to an area you have studied..."

"For a named industry/city/region that you have studied..."

"Use an example in your answer..."

When you use a case study, do not write everything you know about it. Pick out the information that will answer the question, and include facts and figures, place names, specialist terms and labelled sketches or maps.

Oral exams

1. Speak slowly, loudly, clearly and with expression.

2. Listen closely to comments and questions, responding accurately about the topic.

3. Questions/answers will depend on what you have already said, so you can steer the conversation, to a certain extent, towards topics that you prefer.

4. Even if your teacher speaks to you in the familiar *tu* form in French or the *Du* form in German, you should reply in the more formal *vous* or *Sie* form.

5. If you do not understand a question, stay calm and ask the examiner in the foreign language to repeat it. (Prepare this!) If you still do not understand, be honest and say, "I am sorry but I do not understand the question", and the examiner will then rephrase the question or move on to another.

Diagrams

Draw large, clearly labelled diagrams in pencil, then any mistakes can be easily erased and corrected. Graphs need to be clearly marked, so start with a sharply-pointed pencil, always use a rule, and label each axis with the appropriate units. It is also advisable to give graphs, maps and diagrams titles.

In science exams, you may have to draw diagrams of experiments, and you will need to include the diagram of the control (used to check the results of another experiment).

English

Quality not quantity is considered by the exam markers, so a short answer will not be penalised if it contains all the necessary elements. Exam markers want to see:

1. Evidence that you are really familiar with the set texts. This is shown by your knowledge and understanding of plot, character, language, style, setting, and by being able to refer to the text and also quote from it.

2. That you can spell and use interesting and appropriate vocabulary. It's not always the 'difficult' words that are spelled incorrectly; it is often words like 'hear' for 'here' and 'wear' for 'where'.

3. Knowledge of grammar and punctuation. You'd be surprised how many full stops disappear in the heat of the exam room and how many apostrophes end up in the wrong place on the wrong word.

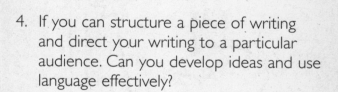

4. If you can structure a piece of writing and direct your writing to a particular audience. Can you develop ideas and use language effectively?

5. That you are able to discuss the author's purpose and audience. Has the author, for example, used certain phrases or words for a particular effect?

6. That you read and understood the question and have planned an answer that deals with each aspect of the question equally.

Now, for some good news! Exam markers understand that your handwriting may deteriorate as you begin to feel the pressure of time. Phew!

Maths and science

These are grouped together because many errors are common to both. If you want to avoid losing unnecessary marks, remember these three points:

1. Be precise – if asked, for example, factors that can affect the growth of the foetus in the womb, it is not enough to just write 'drinking'. You must be more specific and write 'drinking alcohol'.

2. Use appropriate terminology – water when boiled, for example, doesn't 'disappear', it 'evaporates'. As soon as you begin revising, start putting together a glossary of terms and their meanings. Creating your glossary bit by bit is an excellent learning strategy and will give you the confidence to use specialist terms.

3. Full answers – if you leave out the unit
   of measurement, currency or time, for
   example, in your answer, it could be
   deemed as incorrect, ambiguous or
   incomplete. An ambiguous answer is one
   where the examiner is unable to judge
   if you knew the correct answer. An
   ambiguous answer is deemed an
   incorrect answer.

TIPS FROM EXAMINERS ••••••

- Use appropriate terminology.

- Use linking words such as 'therefore', 'however', and 'in contrast'.

- Use every bit of information provided in the question to write a full answer.

- State the obvious and express yourself clearly.

- Use examples and evidence to support your answers or opinions.

- Read questions twice and follow instructions accurately.

- Plan your answers – even short ones – and don't cheat yourself of marks by providing the bare minimum. Make a full answer your target.

- Double-check workings out and make sure you have indicated the correct units of measurement (litres, metres per second, joules, pounds, etc.) and put in decimal points when necessary.

125

- Be clear about the difference between cause and effect. (Cars cause pollution; pollution has an effect on trees.)

- Take a breath and think about your answer before putting pen to paper.

CHAPTER 7

ARE YOU STRESSED?

The exam period is probably the most stressful phase of your life so far. The pressure of revision, the fear of failure, school and parental expectations and uncertainty about college, university or job prospects are probably worrying you, but how are you coping with it? Find out by completing the following quiz.

This stress quiz was complied by **learn.co.uk** and can be found at **www.learn.co.uk/revision/**

1. When you think about your exams, you....

A) ... wonder what all the fuss is about. There's plenty of time. Revision can wait!

B) ... feel a bit disorganised. You haven't stuck to your revision plan and some subjects are weaker than others.

C) ... feel sick. You know how useless you are at exams. It doesn't matter how much you've revised because your mind goes blank.

2. When you go to bed at night, you...

A) ... read the TV guide and think about what you want to watch tomorrow night. There was so much good stuff on tonight!

B) ... worry about your exams. You've been revising but it's hard to remember all the things you studied back in September.

C) ... can't get to sleep. Any sleep you get is full of nightmares about missing exams or having to answer impossible questions.

3. As you get ready for school you catch a glimpse of yourself in the mirror. You immediately think...

A) ... how cool you look. Tonight is another big night out!

B) ... how you look a bit tired. This revision is making you irritable, but at least you're getting enough sleep.

C) ... how awful you look. Your hair looks limp and you have more spots than usual.

4. Your friends are taking a night out from revision and invite you to see the latest blockbuster movie. You...

A) ... jump at the opportunity. The exams are still four weeks away.

B) ... hesitate, but go anyway. You've already spent three evenings revising this week and you deserve a break.

C) ... avoid them. There's far too much work to do and you don't know where to begin.

Where do you stand or collapse on the stress scale?

Mostly As

Stress? You don't know the meaning of the word! But if you don't plan a revision timetable soon, you will definitely feel stressed a week before the exams!

Mostly Bs

Congratulations! There's still a lot to do but you have planned your revision and understand the need to keep everything in perspective.

Mostly Cs

You show all the symptoms of a highly stressed individual! Relax by forgetting about work for a while. Physical exercise is an excellent way of refreshing your mind and body.

WHY THE STRESS?

Exam stress is something you're bound to have heard about. But why does it appear more common now than before?

The first reason is that society recognises that stress does exist and cannot be 'treated' simply by telling someone to 'pull yourself together'. A lot more effort is put in today to make sure you know how to deal with stress in a healthy way.

The second reason is that schools are changing. As they are set more demanding targets by the government, many schools are encouraging competition among pupils and fostering an ethos that does not tolerate failure. An outcome of an increasingly competitive situation can be stress.

In addition, there is the job-place emphasis on qualifications. No matter whether your career objectives are modest or high-flying, skills-based or academic, there are relevant qualifications. And with all other things being equal, the applicant with the most or better qualifications often has greater opportunities of career success. Little wonder then that exam time is stressful.

AN ENEMY WITHIN

But there is 'good' and 'bad' stress. Putting yourself under a little bit of pressure can spur you to improved performance. But when the pressure of circumstances exceeds your ability to cope, then stress is your worst enemy. The signs to watch for are:

1. Inability to sleep.
2. Being quiet and withdrawn.
3. Dramatically altered diet and eating patterns.
4. Deep feelings of despair.

Slamming doors, bursting into tears and generally being one enormous pain means you are letting off steam and expressing, however loudly, your frustrations and anger. It's when you close-down and keep your worries bottled up that trouble looms.

ADVICE FROM THE TOP

"The best way to combat stress is to recognise and deal with it. Stress becomes a problem when parents and children handle it by denying its presence or by doing things to reinforce it. Parents imposing a revision schedule, for example, is a sure way of increasing the stress burden."

**Jim Sweetman
(Curriculum expert and writer)**

COPING STRATEGIES

Be chilled, confident, comfortable and in control

This simple phrase sums up the healthiest approach to any situation that could cause stress. Write them down somewhere to remind yourself how to escape any stress frenzy.

Not the end of the world

Keep revision and exams in perspective. You are not alone, nor are you the first to endure the exam season; hundreds of thousands have been there, done it, bought the T-shirt and went on to party.

Down-time

Sleep for at least eight hours a night and guarantee yourself a least an hour a day in which you can truly relax. While you are relaxing, your brain is absorbing and sorting everything you have learned.

Cut the caffeine

Keep to a balanced, healthy diet, and avoid too much junk food and caffeine (e.g. coffee, coke and tea). Caffeine-based drinks can cause stress and induce stomach cramps.

Be kind to yourself

Reward yourself when you have achieved something, no matter how small it may be. Remind yourself how much you've done by crossing topics off your revision list.

Share it

If you're worried about something – it doesn't matter what – talk it over with a friend, family member or a teacher. The sooner you get it off your chest, the sooner a solution will be discovered.

TOP TIPS

While studying and during exams, these simple and quick 'exercises', extracted from *Wise Guides Exam Skills*, will induce a sense of calm that will 'refresh' your attitude to the task at hand.

- Take a breather – Place your hands on your lap so that they are 'floppy' and let your shoulders and elbows drop. Close your eyes and concentrate on breathing slowly and deeply.  Inhale through your nose and exhale through your mouth. Imagine yourself in a favourite place and relax your face muscles until you feel a smile forming. Keep the smile and get back to work. This routine can transform you in one minute!

- Loosen up – Spread your feet a little and place your heels on the floor. Raise and lower toes slowly five times to feel a stretch up the calves.

- Neck stretch – Close your eyes and very gently tilt your head to the left, back to the centre, and then to the right. Hold each position for a count of two and repeat the cycle two or three times. Keep your shoulders down.

- Shoulder curl – Let your arms drop to your sides loosely and roll your shoulders slowly forwards and backwards a couple of times. Let your shoulders curl to the front and rise at the top of the roll, and for your chest to expand at the back of the roll.

- Hands down – When your writing hand tires, put down your pen and let both arms dangle loosely at your sides. Wiggle your fingers to get the circulation going.

- Torso stretch – For a big stretch, fake a yawn and stretch your arms up or out and take a deep breath.

CHAPTER 8

TODAY'S THE DAY

When the day of the exams dawns, staying calm will help you make the most of all your hard work. Prepare by following this advice from Peter Loach (from *Guardian Education*):

1. Be sure you know exactly where and when each paper of each exam is being held.

2. Remember your examining board, centre number, candidate number, and bring your exam slip with you every time. (16-plus exams only.)

3. Arrive on time. You can be disqualified for lateness.

ADVICE FROM THE TOP

"Give yourself plenty of time to get there, you cannot perform at your best if you're stressed before you start."

Jane Florsham
(Senior teacher and educational consultant)

4. Bring the necessary equipment: black or blue pens, plain pencils and colouring pencils, sharpener, rubber, compasses, protractor, calculator and spare batteries, set squares, a reliable watch, tissues, any set texts, and anything else (except your revision notes!) that will make you feel comfortable and confident.

5. Seek advice from your doctor if you suffer from hay fever or any other persistent medical problems. Remember, some painkillers can cause drowsiness.

6. Make sure you eat breakfast. It's important to be alert in exams, and not feel hunger pangs. Foods that have lots of carbohydrates, such as cereals and bread, will give your brain enough energy for the day.

7. Trust yourself. If you've done your revision, you know a lot more than you think.

ADVICE FROM THE TOP

"Never cram immediately before an exam, it will just make you anxious about things you don't know."

**Jane Florsham
(Senior teacher and educational consultant)**

8. You're about to go into the exam and your heart's pounding. So just take a minute to sit by yourself, taking deep breaths and collecting your thoughts. Now all you need to do is go for it! Good luck.

Three things *not* to do immediately before an exam:

➲ Try to memorise anything!
➲ Work yourself and your friends into a frenzy by comparing how much you studied, what you studied, and what you didn't study.
➲ Tell yourself that you are going to botch this exam.

IN THE EXAM

Before you start the actual exam, be sure that you:

1. Listen carefully to the instructions of the invigilator.

2. Make sure the exam is at the right tier or level. If you think you have the wrong paper, tell the invigilator.

3. Fill in the required details – candidate number, for example, on the answer booklet.

4. Know the number of questions you have to answer and check if there are any compulsory questions.

5. Plan your time carefully.

6. Leave time at the end to check over your paper.

YOU MAY START

1. Read through all of the exam paper, marking those questions you feel confident about. It is best to answer these first.

ADVICE FROM THE TOP

"The key to any exam success is confidence. If you feel happy that you know all you can be expected to know, and how to apply that knowledge, you will be fine."

Jane Florsham
(Senior teacher and educational consultant)

2. Before you start answering a question, make sure you understand it thoroughly and underline keywords and symbols. Unless you have been told otherwise, you may write or make notes on the question paper.

151

3. Spend a few minutes planning your answer in rough. In maths exams, you should show all your workings out.

4. Write as quickly but as legibly as you can. Take care with your spelling.

5. Draw large, clearly labelled diagrams in pencil. Mark graphs with the correct units and always use a ruler to draw straight lines.

6. Set out the stages of experiments in a logical sequence under the appropriate headings.

7. Spend longer answering questions with more marks.

8. Do not speak or hand anything to anyone while in the examination hall, even at the end of an exam. A simple misunderstanding could lead to disqualification. If you need to use the toilet, you should put up your hand – a teacher or invigilator will then go with you.

EMERGENCY TIPS • • • • • • • • • •

Everyone at some time during an exam gets the feeling they have forgotten everything they have learned and revised. For one awful moment (though, at the time this moment seems to drag on like a triple maths lesson!) your mind goes blank. Two seconds ago you knew the answer; now you know nothing, zero, zilch!

The most important thing to do is **NOT PANIC**. A mini panic attack will freeze up the system even more. Instead, try to calm down by doing one of the exercises in Chapter 7. Then use one of the following methods to unblock the memory bank:

- Who? What? When? Where? Why? and How? – ask yourself these questions. For example: Who was involved? When did it occur? How did events unfold? Why did it happen?

- Picture the page – close your eyes and then mentally drag up a picture of your revision notes, class notes or textbook. Flip to the relevant page and scan it to spot the material you need. The more memorable your revision notes, the easier it is to use this memory trick.

- Starts with ... – this is one of the oldest memory prompts around. Go through the alphabet asking yourself if the word started with a, b, c, etc.

- Sounds like, looks like – if the previous prompt hasn't worked, try to imagine how the word sounded or what it looked like. Was it a soft word like 'purr' or a hard word like 'yuk'? Was it a long or short word? Did it have lots of round letters like 'oodles' or tall letters as in 'little'? These may sound like desperate devices, but they do work.

- Look around – raise your eyes from your paper and look at where you are. Take in the view, check out the peeling layers of paint on the ceiling, but make sure it doesn't look as though you are trying to gain inspiration from a mate's paper! Simply taking your mind off the paper for a couple of seconds may jog the missing information from its hiding place.

- Check out the paper – you can sometimes find the very word you want or a piece of related information on the exam question paper.

ADVICE FROM THE TOP

"Think about the context in which you first learned something. Visualise, for example, the science experiment, the methods you used and the results recorded."

Jane Florsham
(Senior teacher and educational consultant)

The most important thing to hold onto during an exam is your confidence. Don't let a question rattle you – you are bigger than any question and have huge inner resources to deal with it. As the American inventor Thomas Edison said: "If we all did the things we're capable of doing, we would literally astound ourselves!"

WANT TO KNOW MORE?

Look out for these other titles developed in association with **learn.co.uk**:

Top Websites for Homework
by Kate Brookes
The first ever pocket guide to the best websites for homework. More and more students are using the Internet as a rich source of information for their homework. This book provides you with an invaluable shortcut to dozens of the most useful websites. All you have to do is look up the school subject, and take your pick. Addresses and short descriptions are provided for each recommended site.

Homework Sorted by Kate Brookes

An essential pocket-sized guide to better homework. *Homework Sorted!* shows you how to get organised – deciding where and when to work, getting the right equipment and planning study time effectively. It's also packed with time-saving advice on finding the information you need, including useful organisations and websites recommended by **learn.co.uk**. All presented in easily digestible chunks and a reassuring style - SORTED!

Other titles by Hodder
Children's Books

the txt book by Kate Brookes
The best text message book ever! All the abbreviations, acronyms and similes you will ever need, together with lots of hints on expert texting. Packed with essential messages for all aspects of life, together with a few to make you giggle...

Little Book of Exam Skills by Kate Brookes
Prepare yourself for exams with this little book. It's packed with brilliant revision tips you can start using *right now* – plus top exam techniques to help you make the grade!

Little Book of Exam Calm by Anita Naik
Keep your cool at exam time with the help of this little book. Packed with advice on how to stay happy and healthy before and during your exams, it will provide you with a calm and confident route to exam success!

You can buy all these books from your local bookseller, or order them direct from the publisher. For more information, write to:

The Sales Department, Hodder Wayland, a division of Hodder Headline Limited, 338 Euston Road, London, NW1 3BH.

Visit our website at
www.madaboutbooks.com

REVISION
SORTED!

Kate Brookes

**Developed in
association with**

a division of Hodder Headline Limited